My Animals & Other Family

Novels
The Book of Colour
The Leper's Companion

Non-Fiction
Charles Waterton
The Emperor's Last Island
Daisy Bates in the Desert
Old Man Goya
With Billie

illustrated by
Herman Makkink

Julia Blackburn

My Animals
&
Other Family

JONATHAN CAPE
LONDON

Published by Jonathan Cape 2007

2 4 6 8 10 9 7 5 3 1

Copyright © Julia Blackburn 2007

Author has asserted her right under the Copyright, Designs
and Patents Act 1988 to be identified as the author of this work

First published in Great Britain in 2007 by Jonathan Cape
Random House, 20 Vauxhall Bridge Road,
London SW1V 2SA

www.rbooks.co.uk

Addresses for companies within The Random House Group Limited can be found at:
www.randomhouse.co.uk/offices.htm

The Random House Group Limited Reg. No. 954009

A CIP catalogue record for this book
is available from the British Library

ISBN 9780224082341

The Random House Group Limited makes every effort to ensure that the papers used in its books
are made from trees that have been legally sourced from well-managed and credibly certified forests.
Our paper procurement policy can be found at: www.rbooks.co.uk/environment

Printed and bound in Germany by
GGP Media GmbH, Pößneck

For Natasha, Martin & Fiona

My Animals & Other Family

A Bushbaby from Harrods

I have two photographs of him. In the first photograph he stands on Great-Aunt Molly's chest of drawers, his arms wrapped around the neck of a bottle of Jamaican rum. Four Barrels rum, and the picture on the label shows a group of men and women being happy on a sugar plantation. He and the bottle are about the same size, although if he stretched his legs to their full length, he would be a bit taller. There is a triumphant look in his round, night-time eyes; he must be slightly drunk, from having licked traces of rum from the edges of the screw-top.

In the second photograph I am sitting in an armchair which also belonged to Great-Aunt Molly and he is perched on my shoulder. We are both staring straight into the lens of the camera. I am eleven years old, plump and uncertain and wearing a pale blue sundress with white polka dots which has grown too small for me. The little

I am eleven years old, plump and uncertain

curl at the end of his tail hangs down across the tight bodice of the dress.

It's a good-quality photograph, done by a professional. She came to the house with flashlights and tripods to make a portrait of my father for a book cover and then she wandered around and took other pictures as well. In this one you can see the flashlights reflected in his eyes, the softness of his fur which gave his body a misty outline and the little pads on his delicate fingers, each one tipped with a perfect fingernail. You can also see that I am shining with happiness in spite of being plump and uncertain, because I am in love and the object of my love is there, on my shoulder.

Congo was a bushbaby. I called him Congo because of a poem. I could always learn poetry very easily and so my father taught me huge chunks of it, pretty much as soon as I could speak. I had just started going to Bennett Road County Primary School in Leeds, where Mr Pepper the Headmaster gave us a weekly talk on the dangers of litter, when my father taught me a poem called 'The Congo', written by the nineteenth-century American poet Vachel Lindsay:

> *Then I saw the Congo creeping through the black,*
> *Cutting through the jungle with a golden track.*
> *Then along that river bank*
> *A thousand miles*
> *Tattooed cannibals danced in files.*

It didn't matter that Congo the bushbaby had been snatched from the forests of Madagascar rather than the jungles of Africa; the name evoked my idea of tall trees and the darkness of his natural home.

He was given to me by a friend of my father's, a woman called Erica Marx who ran the Hand and Flower poetry press. She came to our house for tea, took one look at me and decided I needed companionship. So I received a letter: a single sheet of thick, creamy paper and instead of an address at the top, there was a drawing of a hand with a flower growing out of it. 'Dear Julia,' said the letter. 'I want you to go to Harrods and choose yourself a pet. Any pet you like and don't worry how much it costs.'

I had never been to Harrods in my life because we weren't Harrodsy people, but off I went now, by bus. I pushed through the heavy swing doors and into the shock and glitter of the perfume department. Then up in the lift to the second floor and there, sandwiched between Pianos and Carpets, was the Zoo.

I recently contacted the man in the Archive Department at Harrods and he sent me a selection of old advertisements and magazine articles about the Zoo in the 1950s. This was a time when coral reefs were still thriving and jungles were not being reduced to ashes and nobody was going to question the morality of buying a two-toed sloth or an eighty-pound Malay bear if that was what you wanted. A press handout explained that 'English and foreign royalty, film, stage and TV stars, millionaires, MPs and visiting Americans are among the Zoo's regular customers … One well-known Marchioness paused to look around and

sandwiched between Pianos and Carpets

bought a five-guinea bullfrog. A customer enquiring about Siamese cats got a Toucan instead …'

For me, as the child I then was, the Harrods Zoo was as close as I had ever been to heaven. I walked slowly past the rows of cages, pens and tanks peering at their occupants in a daze of desire. The air was loud with the cries of parrots and small birds, thick with the scent of fur and faeces.

After a while I narrowed my choice down to a mongoose or a bushbaby. I had read the story of Rikki-tikki-tavi, so I knew that a mongoose would lay down his life for me if there was ever a cobra in our bathroom, but I chose the bushbaby, for the way he uncurled himself and stared straight at me when the assistant picked him up and placed him in my hands.

I took him home on the bus in a cardboard box lined with hay to keep out the cold London air. The cardboard box also contained a tin of live mealworms, those yellow scaly maggoty creatures that live on bran and make a rustling sound as they go about the business of doing what they do. I had instructions to feed my bushbaby on

7

chopped fruit, Nestlé's sweetened condensed milk and about four mealworms a day.

There was a room next to my bedroom that was too small and narrow to be used for anything much, a sort of appendix in the body of the house. It had a window looking out on to the garden and it contained little more than a sink, a tottering pile of old *National Geographic* magazines and a heap of my father's climbing ropes. A discarded fur coat of my mother's was draped over a hook on the door and an old cloth cap that must have once belonged to my father was perched on top of it. This room was given to Congo and during the daylight hours when he wanted to sleep he would climb up the soft fur of the coat and post himself into the little hollow of the cap.

From the moment he came to live with me, my whole world took on a different shape and focus. I almost forgot about the problems of family life. If my father got drunk and came home coughing his chiming-clock cough that meant he was looking for trouble, then I hardly noticed the fights and shouts that were sure to follow. And if my

a sort of appendix in the body of the house

mother wept and said she wished she had a husband who loved her and who was faithful to her, I no longer felt that my fragile world of family was about to collapse and I must do something to save it. I had my own life now, my own independent existence.

I'd come home from school at four o'clock, just when Congo's nocturnal day was ready to begin. Sometimes he was already awake, or else I would lift the cap from the coat to watch him uncurling himself, yawning, and blinking and eager to get started. I'd put him on my shoulder and he would gently pull a curtain of my hair to one side so that he could grasp my ear and explore it with his nose, licking my skin, feeling the contours of my face with his small hands.

My mother's studio was next to my bedroom. It was a big room which also served as a sitting room, so as well as an easel and a table covered with tubes of paint and brushes and a wooden rack stacked with paintings there was also a sofa and the mahogany chest of drawers. Every space on the walls was covered with my mother's paintings, which were hung on long wires descending from one of those old-fashioned wooden picture rails that ran all around the room, about fifteen inches from the ceiling.

The studio became an urban jungle. Congo could leap from my hand to the easel, from the easel to the chest of drawers and then from the chest of drawers up onto the open highway of the picture rail. Like a tiny kangaroo, he would bounce on his long hind legs round and round the upper layer of the room, his tail poised in a balancing curve. And if I called him, he would stop at the sound of my voice, gaze down at me, fold up the catapulting energy of his long legs and leap out in a great arc to land on my outstretched hand, as soft as an answered wish.

After a while, every room in our ramshackle house took on the sweet and musty smell of bushbaby. Thanks to the picture-rail highway, the wallpaper in the studio, as well as the paintings themselves, were soon streaked with long thin stains where Congo's pee had trickled down. And there were little grape-seed piles of excrement on every available surface: on the chest of drawers, on the

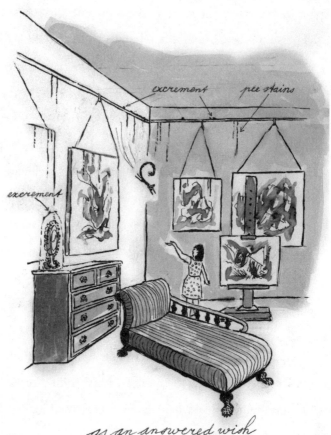

excrement   pee stains

excrement

as an answered wish

back of the old chaise longue with its Empire stripes and even clinging to the glass dome of the clock which some sombre Huguenot ancestor was said to have brought with him to England while escaping persecution in France. I suppose guests must have found the overriding presence of a bushbaby a bit disconcerting, but my parents were far too busy with their battles to notice and I was too much in love to be bothered by such details.

I think it was my mother who, in spite of her own experience of the perils of matrimony, decided that Congo needed a wife. And so we got a second bushbaby and I called her Liana, after the dangling jungle vines that I felt she must have once grasped in her hands. She was much bigger than Congo and it was immediately apparent that she belonged to a very different variety of the species. The two of them had little in common. True, they slept wrapped in each other's arms and tails in their cloth-cap nest, but that was the limit of their relationship. Congo continued with his evening social life, while Liana spent all her time in bed. Every day I would persuade her to eat a bit of fruit and crunch a few mealworms, but although she kept healthy she had no interest in this alien world she had been brought to and she never lost her look of homesickness, reproach and despair.

That summer we went on a week's holiday to Cornwall and a family friend agreed to stay in our house to look after the bushbabies. We took ropes and climbing shoes because that was what we did on all our holidays. We slept in a building belonging to the Climbers' Club and each morning we set off up granite cliff faces, threaded together on a length of nylon rope, like three beads on a string. My father led the way, chain smoking and grunting, but happy to be back on the rocks, I came next and my mother followed behind.

'Come along, darling, there's a ledge just a bit further to your left.'

'I can't reach it!'

And then my mother's voice. 'She can't reach it!'

'Yes she can!'

'No I can't!'

like three
beads
on a string

15

'Look, she's managed it. I said you could, darling. I'll secure the belay while your mother comes up.'

The seven days of our holiday were soon over. We were driving home and I was sitting in the back seat of our Austin Princess with its odd rubbery smells. My mother turned to me and said she had some bad news. The friend who had been staying in our house had telephoned: one of the bushbabies had died.

'Congo or Liana?'

'I don't know.'

How terrible to be wanting one death in preference to another. To be reciting a little circular prayer as the car rattled its way towards London: 'Dear God, if you are anywhere and if you are listening, let it be Liana who has died.'

But it was Congo. The window had been left open a tiny bit and he must have stood there in the darkness of the night, staring at the trees and the northern stars while the cold air crept across his belly and entered him and took his life.

I buried him in the rose bed. I kept Liana for a few weeks, but she became sadder than ever and so I gave her to the Lesser Mammals Department at the London Zoo. In return I received a free entry pass which lasted for a year.

At that time the Lesser Mammals were kept in a solemn red-brick building that could have served as the waiting room for a Victorian railway station. The daylight streamed in through the tall windows, and as a result all the nocturnal animals remained fast asleep during visiting hours.

There was not much more to see than bundles of rounded backs, softly breathing fur and perhaps the occasional blinking eye. But I can still remember the mixture of sadness and joy that overwhelmed me when I entered that room. I would go straight to the cages that contained the sleeping bushbabies, crouch down on my knees and press my face as close as I could to the wire mesh. Then I would take a deep breath, to inhale that sweet and bitter, musty fruity earthy smell deep into my

to inhale that fruity earthy smell

lungs. And with that all the memories of the first great love of my life would come rushing back.

Tortoises and Tropical Fish

Imust have collected money somehow, pocket money perhaps, and when we went to visit my grandparents, the ones in Hove, then just as we were saying our goodbyes – my father tight-lipped and bobbing up and down with eagerness to be gone – my grandfather would suddenly grasp hold of my hand and prise the fingers open and press a hot half-crown into the palm. So, I had money to buy things and what I bought mostly was tropical fish.

The tropical fish tank was in my bedroom, resting its great weight on the chest of drawers. It was an old tank and little rivulets of rusty water were always finding their way into my knicker-and-sock drawer. There was a sheet of glass on top of it, and a simple metal light fitment with a 25-watt bulb sat on the glass. I never had one of those aerating systems that create a gurgling blanket of sound in doctors' waiting rooms, but when the balance of life was right, it worked beautifully: a luminous oasis of trailing, floating, spiralling plants, through which all sorts of fish moved and had their being.

Most Saturday mornings I'd set off with an empty jam jar and an old woollen sock and I'd make my way to the shop that sold tropical fish. Down the road and then first right, past the lugubrious church run by the Reverend Hope who lived with Mrs Hope and their family of little Hopes in the house next to ours. Godfrey Hope was the same age as me but much smaller and whenever he was nervous or caught telling a lie then his eyes would blink at a tremendous speed. He came into our house once and saw the Tibetan Buddha sitting poised and smiling on its wooden stand on the mantelpiece. 'Is that a heathen god?' he asked, his eyelids flickering as fast as the needle on my mother's Singer sewing machine. 'My father says you are all heathens.'

So, past the church and then left, down to the poor end of the high street, the road getting dirtier and sadder, and there on a corner was the painted sign proclaiming, 'Tropical Fish'.

"Is that a heathen god?" asked Godfrey Hope

The lady who owned the shop was small and wispy; she had her grey hair in a bun and she wore a flowered apron. I used to wonder if it was her husband's shop and then he had died and she had taken over without really wanting to. The narrow room was crowded with rows of tanks and she would sigh mournfully as she tried to catch a particular fish with a soft net. I don't remember ever seeing other customers there.

I loved the daze that took possession of me the moment I walked into that shop; it was like breathing in some soporific drug. I would drift from tank to tank, from the shoals of zebra fish moving in perfect unison, to the nervous, luminous neons and the gentle-faced, flat-bodied gouramis with their tendency to eat anything smaller than themselves. Black widows, platties, mollies, angel fish, leopard eels, and the wonderful Siamese fighters, their trailing tails and fins like shot silk in reds and purples. Best of all I loved the catfish, for their whiskery moustaches and the look of embarrassed surprise in their round eyes as they worked like little vacuum cleaners on the gravel floor, standing on their heads and sucking up all the rubbish they could find. Catfish were not glamorous, but they were good at surviving. I remember a disastrous power cut which snatched the colour and the life out of all of my fishes, except for that one determined and bewhiskered gentleman.

Sometimes I would simply stare into the tanks and buy nothing, or nothing more than a pennyworth of those clumps of red tubifex worms that tropical fish find so delicious, or a bag of fearful, bouncing water fleas that did their hopeless best to avoid capture when you tipped them en masse into the tank. If I was getting a new fish, it took ages to decide on one in particular and then the shop lady would sigh and mutter as she hunted it down and flipped it into my jam jar and helped me to pull the sock over the jar to keep the water warm. I walked home clutching my prize, with as little bounce as possible in each step.

I suppose tropical fish were my religion. I had tried prayer – 'Lighten-our-darkness-we-beseech-Thee-O-Lord-and-by-Thy-great-mercy-defend-us-from-all-

I suppose tropical fish were my religion

perils-and-dangers-of-this-night-amen'– but even as I prayed I could hear the perils and dangers of my father's shouts and my mother's screams. For a while I'd thought that maybe I needed to suffer some more, in order to make contact with a benevolent Almighty, and so I'd go out into the frightening dark of the garden and kneel on the stones of the path and press my fingers into my eyelids until I could see the heavens open above me. Nothing changed and the fights got worse. Eventually I gave up on God.

But I performed something like prayer in front of the fish tank. I knelt there and stared into that silent world and slowly my racing heart would settle into a more steady rhythm and I would feel comforted.

I must have sometimes been still for an hour or more. I can remember the shock of returning to the reality of my room and how stiff my legs were when I got to my feet.

Years later, long after I had left home, I discovered that tortoises were also good for quieting a racing heart. I was living in Amsterdam and I had a job which involved making a weekly list of cultural events for a magazine called *Holland Today Yesterday and Tomorrow.* That paid for rent and food and gave me hours and hours of time in which to drift and worry and wonder what I was doing with my life.

One day I went to the Zoo. I headed straight for the Aquarium, but it didn't work for me like the fish tank in my childhood bedroom; the building was too enclosed, too dark, it was too much like going to the cinema with the fish flickering across the screen of their Technicolor tanks.

So I went to the Reptile House instead. Sunlight streamed in through the glass panels in the roof and the air was hot and damp. There were several watery pens containing crocodiles and alligators smiling in their sleep, as if dreaming terrible dreams. And next to them, the tortoise compound: a little world of slowness and quietness in which a mixed collection of tortoises and terrapins ate and slept and dipped into shallow water and took ponderous steps in one short direction or another.

I leant on the wooden railing and looked down on tortoises. I examined the swirling landscape of tortoise shells. I watched the slow process of yawning, the effort of eating a single lettuce leaf.

The lack of sudden movement meant that I could study all those tortoise faces and they kept reminding me of my grandfather, he of the hot half-crown. Towards the end of his life he became very reptilian, sitting silently in an armchair in a nursing home, staring and gulping and every so often yawning to reveal a heavy pink tongue, just like that of a tortoise. He also had the same sad dark tortoise eyes.

I started talking with the keeper of the Reptiles. He was called Mr van Morsel and he said he was very pleased to meet someone who wanted to spend time with his tortoises. He told me that if I came to the back door of the Reptile House any morning around eight I could go and sit with the tortoises in their compound, until the official opening time of nine thirty.

they kept reminding me of my grandfather

I went there regularly for several weeks. Mr van Morsel told me I could ride on the back of one of the big Galapagos tortoises, and so very carefully I perched on that ancient carapace, letting myself be carried a short distance across the sand. He warned me against a smaller yellow-shelled member of the tribe who might try to ram the underside of his shell against my leg if I wasn't careful. He told me that if a tortoise escapes from captivity, it will always set off in an easterly direction, towards Mecca.

And then I was back in London and working for a book publisher who was producing a short history of the world. It was a strange job: all the events and discoveries and achievements of human life had to be boiled down into a minimal number of words and then fitted into columns. I was busy with the ancient Greeks.

At that time I was living with my long-ago husband in an abandoned tea warehouse close to the Thames. The space we rented had been used for tasting the different blends of tea. There was a big area under a skylight where the tea chests had been lined up and a little glass-panelled office where endless cups of tea had been prepared. They must have taken it in sips and then spat it out because there were dark tea stains on the floor and on the walls of the office. I found an old ledger which recorded the batches of tea tasted between 1930 and 1939, at which point there was a shaky line drawn across the page in ink, followed by the words, 'Work terminated, due to outbreak of War.'

In those days most of the warehouses were empty and nothing was locked, so you could simply pull back the heavy bolts on the doors that divided one abandoned building from the next and explore the succession of dim spaces. I remember a vast area filled with rags bound up in cubes, each cube as tall as a man; a warehouse that had been used for storing butter, the walls lined with a red pine wood, glistening as if it was alive. I remember going down through a door and entering a canteen: plates and cups and drying-up cloths and a sense that a whole crowd of men and women had simply walked away and forgotten to return.

I felt happy in a rather remote way. I felt at home. And as if to prove the point, I set up a tropical fish tank on a table inside that glass-panelled Victorian office. I bought a bag of washed gravel, a couple of bunches of the grassy valerian plants, and a pair of the most easy-going of tropical fish, the guppy. The male has long trailing tails decorated with little bursts of colour; the female, three times as big as her husband, is ponderous and plain but confident in the certainty of being desired. And I bought a catfish, to bustle about and keep things in order.

There they were, the three of them, busy with the tiny preoccupations of their lives, and I would spend long stretches of abstracted time, just watching them.

My father came to see me at the warehouse. It was his one and only visit. I heard him clanging up the metal steps and then he walked slowly into that big space with its industrial grey light and stood there, awkward and uncertain. He was wearing a white linen suit which had become far too tight for him. He was carrying a black leather briefcase, which made him look very academic, even though he'd given up teaching a couple of years previously, due to ill health. I had presumed the briefcase must contain books or papers, although when he finally opened its wide mouth, it was filled to the brim with cans of Long Life beer. He always drank that beer because he liked the name.

I took him by the hand and led him to the tropical fish tank. I asked if he remembered how I used to have a tank like this when I was a child. He grunted and said, 'Yes, darling.' For a while we sat side by side in silence, staring at the guppy husband and wife, and at the catfish being busy.

'Glad you've got a catfish,' he said eventually. 'I always liked the catfish best.' And then, 'Good to see you looking well. It can't have been easy, your childhood, but you've got through OK and that's what matters.'

It was nice. I don't think he'd ever talked so much about the past before. He tipped his cans of beer onto the table and set them in a line and drank them one by one, and then he was gone, clattering back down the metal fire-escape steps and wandering out into the streets of London in a daze of Long Life. I continued to sit in front of my little fish tank and the catfish watched me with its round and humorous eye.

He set them in a line and drank them one by one

Chickens, Guinea Pigs and the Facts of Life

Plovdiv is a good name for a guinea pig, but then there are so many good names for guinea pigs: Kafka, Orangeade, Mephistopheles, though perhaps Mephistopheles is more suitable for a cockerel. I sometimes think the main reason for keeping guinea pigs, and chickens too, is because they can have so many babies and every baby needs a name.

We once had a wild and skinny bantam – Tufty Top – who hatched seven chicks in a well-hidden nest under a rose bush. They were known as Monday, Tuesday, Wednesday, Thursday, Friday, Saturday and Sunday. And then, not long after the hatching there was a terrible thunderstorm and Monday and Tuesday got rained away, while Wednesday must have been hit on the head by the weight of the raindrops because she was never quite all there. She became known as Wednesday Afternoon.

Back to guinea pigs. Guinea pigs were responsible for

FluffBum

Plovdiv

Kafka

Orangeade

Mephistopheles

teaching me the facts of life as I wished to know them. At school, a school for girls where we wore purple uniforms and straw hats in summer and felt hats in winter and two pairs of knickers all through the year, we were taught about sex in a single biology lesson.

We had finished tapeworms with their hooked and helmeted heads, their suckers and their segments, we had done the carefree and adaptable existence of single-celled amoeba, and then suddenly we were hurtled into rabbits and the technicalities of reproduction.

Miss Herring, who later married Mr Fisher, steered a squeaking piece of chalk into a drawing of a womb with its two elegant Fallopian branches, the ova poised in what looked like eggcups at the end of each branch. There was a brief explanation of the process of fertilisation, gestation and birth. 'It's the same with humans,' said Miss Herring, turning pink. I remember she also turned pink in a scripture lesson when she accidentally tumbled us head first into the middle of the Book of Genesis and the doomed cities of Sodom and Gomorrah.

"It's the same with humans"
said Miss Herring, turning pink

What Miss Herring didn't realise was that as a school guinea pig monitor, I already knew about the facts of life. I had been taught how to press very gently at the base of a soft, hay-smelling tummy, in order to discover if I was holding a male or a female. I had witnessed copulation and birth and knew how to feel the number of babies being carried in a tiny womb. Because I was responsible for controlling the guinea-pig population, I was aware of guinea-pig passion and how a male will let out his gudda-gudda-gudda cry of desire and will even mate with his wife half an hour after the delivery of three or four perfect, wide-eyed babies, if he gets the chance. And I knew that if I failed to stop that urgent hustling piggyback ride, then another batch of babies was due in nine and a half weeks' time.

Once my childhood was over, there followed many long years without the company of guinea pigs, until the day when my three-year-old daughter was presented with a large, fat, smooth-haired member of the guinea-pig tribe, who bore the name of Galaxy.

Galaxy was a bachelor and he became my daughter's companion pretty well everywhere she went. He travelled in his own hay-filled basket, for visits to friends, shopping expeditions or car journeys. He would sit there comfortably eating a carrot or a slice of apple, but was quick to respond if he was picked up and talked to. My daughter would leave him lying about, as you would a book, and I sometimes found him patiently marooned on the kitchen table among the remains of breakfast, on a pile of Sunday newspapers, or even on the top of the record player or eating washed lettuce in the empty sink. On these adventures, he never tried to escape, and if you called for him he would answer, in much the same voice as a cordless telephone that lets out a little ringing cry from wherever it has last been abandoned.

When my daughter had just started going to school, she developed a close friendship with a ninety-nine-year-old lady called Dorothy. Dorothy spent her days as well as her nights, propped up in a high bed in the house of her son and daughter-in-law. She had been a great beauty and she still had the confidence of that knowledge. Her fingernails were perfectly manicured and painted bright red. Her long hair was spread on her pillow like the hair of a princess.

My daughter would arrive with all the friendly bustle and chatter of a district nurse, carrying Galaxy in her shopping basket. She would clamber up onto Dorothy's bed and then the two of them, separated by almost a hundred long years, would talk guinea pig.

During these conversations, Dorothy often drifted back to a past time when people arrived by carriage and there were servants keeping things in order downstairs.

'Who is this little girl? Did the coachman bring her?' she would enquire.

'Don't be silly, Dorothy. You know who I am. I'm me and I've brought Galaxy.'

'Galaxy? Am I acquainted with a Galaxy?'

'Of course you are, here he is. We can stroke him together.' And then they would sit side by side and stroke Galaxy and Galaxy would answer their attentions

"Am I acquainted with a Galaxy?"

by tossing his stubby head and letting out little cries of appreciation.

We had moved from London to an old farmhouse in the country surrounded by a rambling garden, and with this change of life it was felt that Galaxy could have a wife. FluffBum was her name: a beautiful maiden with long sweeps of honey-coloured fur.

As soon as she was presented to him, Galaxy, who had always been the mildest of creatures, let out a shriek and began the gudda-gudda-gudda sound of guinea-pig passion. He leapt from my daughter's hands and even bit her thumb in his haste.

Galaxy and his young bride went to live in the garden. They had a cage, with a sleeping compartment filled with hay, but the cage door was left open. After a while, and with the addition of more guinea pigs brought in from outside, Galaxy became the king of a multicoloured nation. As well as several open-doored cages, there were also new housing developments under the tumbling remains of an outside latrine.

Some of the younger generation became a bit wild and unbiddable, but Galaxy never forgot his roots. You could stand in the garden and call the guinea-pig cry of whee-whee-whee-whee and from far away, under the apple tree, or by the pond, or on the mound of earth that was left over from digging a cesspit where curly kale grew so well, came the answering cry. And like a little train, he would come trundling towards you as fast as his short legs could take him.

One day I heard that cry, but higher pitched than usual and more urgent. I went in search of the sound and there was Galaxy, racing through the grass with a weasel riding on his back and biting into his neck. I shouted at the weasel with as much anger and authority as I could muster. For one crucial moment it let go of its grip and Galaxy was able to escape. Then, and I'll never forget this, the weasel turned on me. It reared up to its full height like a snake or a mongoose, and it swayed backwards and forwards, staring me in the eye and shrieking with rage.

A couple of years passed and one morning, my daughter

Galaxy became the king
of a multi-coloured nation

came into the kitchen cradling Galaxy in her arms. She held him up to me and said, 'There's something wrong with him.' She was right, there was something wrong with him, he was dead. I didn't know how to explain this other fact of life to her, how to say that there is sleep, and there is also the endless sleep.

And chickens? In that same farm of my children's childhood, so different from the city flats and houses of my childhood, we had free-range chickens as well as free-range guinea pigs. Riff Raff, the cockerel, shimmering with metallic lights and every bit as fine as Chaucer's Chanticleer, and a mixed collection of very wild and independent bantams. Some, like Tufty Top, had feathers sprouting incongruously from the crowns of their heads, giving them a look of permanent surprise; others had a mass of feathers sprouting between their toes. We also had a big black-and-white speckled Maron hen called Boaty, who was sitting complacently on a dark brown egg when she was given to us. That egg became Young Boaty, and mother and daughter could never bear to be separated for a moment so they even hatched chicks together on the same nest. This harem of ladies were all competing with each other for Riff Raff's attention.

Riff Raff was courteous with each of them, but Tufty Top was his particular favourite. He would find a worm or something as good as a worm, and make a noise of strangulated surprise, addressed to her alone. The others would gather up their fluffy petticoats and come running to see what was on offer, but it was only Tufty Top who was being called. And while she was busy with the worm, Riff Raff would mount her in a flurry of feathers and the other hens would watch and gossip about it afterwards.

Chickens are always busy with the drama of life. One hen announces she has laid an egg and there is a great chorus of excitement as the others celebrate her achievement. One hen thinks she has seen a hawk and gives a warning cry and they all cry the same warning. And like other domestic animals that have had a long association with people, they want to get closer and closer still to the human world. Ours would stand outside the door, waiting for the opportunity to march as solemn as penguins into the kitchen where they felt their true home should be. Or they would balance on the window ledge and peck at the glass with a look of longing in their round eyes.

We had a peaceable kingdom. And then, for a while, we had foxes. These were two orphaned foxcubs that had been found washed up into a heap of bedragglement by a riverbank. My daughter looked after them. She called them Lily and Rothko and kept them in a little hut at one end of the garden and fed them on baby milk formula for the first couple of weeks. When they needed real food with bones and feathers and fur they were provided with the occasional fresh dead pheasant or rabbit found on the road, or, failing that, with day-old chicks from a chicken farm nearby.

The foxes grew and flourished. They got faster and fatter and more and more foxy, the smell of them as sharp as knives. At first my daughter kept them inside and they would climb over her when she went to feed them, mewling like cats. Then she got two little harnesses for them and long leads and took them out into the fields to smell the earth and the air and get used to the world. Like identical twins they shared the same instants of thought and movement, both leaping, turning, and stopping in the same choreographed instant.

Then the day came on which they wanted their freedom. Early in the morning we heard them in the hut, yammering with desperation. The moment the door was open, instead of waiting to be harnessed, they burst out into the garden like two red flames, flickering with energy.

They were there among the chickens. And the chickens, who had got used to landing on the back of our docile dog and treating him as if he were a furry relative, went to inspect the foxes. The oppressors and the oppressed stared at each other with mild curiosity. The chickens made small noises of surprise and the foxes sniffed at their feathers and sneezed and looked bemused. For a brief few minutes

like identical twins

I entered a state of suspended disbelief. For a brief few minutes I thought that the patterns of nature were not fixed: the lion could after all lie down with the lamb and all would be well. There was no need for war or bloodshed in this world.

Then Tufty Top made a sudden movement and the spell was broken. The foxes woke up from their quiet dream and lunged at her. They got a mouthful of feathers, but Tufty Top escaped, shrieking with shock and righteous indignation. The others scattered and flew up with a clattering of wings into the low branches of the oak tree where they roosted at night. Two of them fell back and that was the end of them.

We managed to corral the foxes back into their hut before they discovered the guinea pigs. On the morning of the next day, we persuaded them into a large straw basket and took them in the car to a wood not far from the sea and there we released them. They wandered off rather vaguely, looking wistfully over their shoulders as they went.

A few weeks later I was told that a school party had gone for a picnic and two charming foxes had arrived to watch them and to share their sandwiches.

the lion could lie down with the lamb

Two Very Different Dogs

My bushbaby was long gone. I had Pedro, the marmalade cat, but he was nonchalant in his manner and tended to scratch. I had tropical fish and there were guinea pigs at school, but what I really needed was a dog. A dog is faithful and true and noble and brave and trusting and kind. A dog fetches sticks and guards the house and growls at robbers, or at anyone else who might threaten the happiness of the family.

Family happiness was not something we had much of, but both my mother and father agreed that a dog was a good idea. So, I was given a puppy: a black cocker spaniel wriggling with hope and uncertainty. His official name was Trigger Glory, but I called him Jason, even though there was nothing golden about his fleece.

Jason's silky coat fell into rivulets of curls. His wide, sensible feet had fluffy bits between the toes and his huge rubbery nose was like an independent creature, twitching and shivering under the bombardment of smells that came at it from all sides.

He arrived with a stiff piece of paper – rather like a guarantee for an electric appliance – which showed that he was descended from a noble line of ancestors, all of whom had been brought up in accordance with the rules of hunting and good behaviour.

Jason was genetically programmed to be obedient. I only had to say, 'Here!' and he was beside me waiting for further instructions. 'Heel!' and like Good King Wenceslas's servant he followed so closely in my footsteps that I worried I might knock his chin with the heel of my shoe. If I threw a stick or a ball, he'd wait until I said 'Fetch!' before galumphing off to get it, bring it back and wait for the command to drop it at my feet. Then he'd sit down on his stumpy tail and stare at me, a look of gentle devotion in his sad brown eyes.

I wanted to share everything with Jason. I'd take him in my arms and whisper a great shopping list of my troubles into one of his big flat ears. I'd let my tears drip into his

Jason was genetically programmed

black fur. But, although he was amenable in his way and would seem to listen, I was never sure if he understood the seriousness of what I was telling him.

'You can go anywhere with a dog to protect you,' my parents said, and I agreed. I'd go for long walks in the park, made brave and independent by the presence of my new companion. Jason and I would pad along side by side in a vague but agreeable dream, looking at trees and flowers and birds.

But then, one afternoon, on a bit of the path which was rather narrow and enclosed, I suddenly became aware of a man standing just ahead of us and watching our approach. I wasn't wearing my spectacles so everything was a bit blurred, but I could see that the man's trousers were around his knees and I knew how to recognise trouble even if that trouble was very out of focus.

Jason must have sensed the danger as well, but he didn't growl or bark. I had the rather disconcerting feeling that he was even more afraid than I was. I kept my eyes fixed on the ground and as soon as we had passed the man, I

trouble out of focus

began to run, with Jason lolloping close by my side. The man didn't pursue us. After a while we stopped running and headed towards home by a different route.

On our way back, I saw one of the policemen who patrolled the park, riding like the Lone Ranger on a big horse. I waved at him to stop. He reined in his horse and peered down at me benevolently from his great equine height. I told him what had happened.

The Lone Ranger was not impressed. He didn't ask for my name or address. He didn't even suggest that he and his horse might accompany me as far as the main road. All he said was, 'Don't worry, little girl. Only one in ten attacks.' And that was that and he was off, galloping into the distance.

When I got home, I told my mother about the man on the path. She found the story very funny. She wanted to know how old the man was. I then told my father and he was thrilled by the idea of such a potentially dangerous drama. He suggested that together we should go back to the same area, first thing in the morning. I'd stand on the path and be the decoy and he'd hide in the bushes close by. He'd jump out and catch the man and tie him up with a rope, before leading him triumphantly to the police station.

I didn't like the plan. I didn't think anyone from the adult world had been very helpful. I decided that Jason and I must give up going for solitary walks together.

So my father took over the responsibility of exercising the dog. His walks were fast and gruelling excursions, designed to sweat off the alcohol that had accumulated in his body the night before. And if he had drunk more than usual, then he went jogging, dressed in an old anorak even at the height of summer.

In those days nobody jogged and people would stare wide-eyed as he bobbed along. He always followed exactly the same route through the park and sometimes he'd stop to climb into a big oak tree. He'd settle himself like a clumsy bird among the spreading branches and stay there for ages, smoking cigarettes.

Jason did his best. He trotted as well as he could at my

father's heels and if he needed to wait under a tree for a while, then he waited. But the relationship between man and dog began to deteriorate.

It was Jason's good behaviour that made my father so angry. 'He is worse than Rosencrantz and Guildenstern, fawning at my heels,' he said. 'He has no mind of his own. He should be more independent... Your mother is to blame. I'd never have chosen a creature like this.'

My father determined to unlearn the cocker spaniel traditions that he so despised. I'm not sure how he did this, but it was clear that at some point a switch inside Jason's brain was flicked and all of his genetic patterns went into reverse.

Now, instead of following to heel, he would run off in all directions and come back when he chose to. If you threw him a stick, he took the stick in his jaws and held tight. And if you spoke the magic word 'Drop!' he simply held the stick even tighter, while emitting a rasping, gurgling sound and showing his teeth. He also began to growl in defence of pebbles or leaves or any other small and insignificant objects which happened to lie in front of his nose.

The walks in the park became increasingly complicated. By now Jason would growl the moment he saw my father. And so when the two of them went for a walk together, a complicated ritual needed to be followed. My father opened the back door of the car and stepped to one side, waiting at a safe distance while the dog jumped in. Then dog and man would set off, both muttering darkly at each other. The same careful procedure had to be followed in reverse when they arrived at their destination.

It seems absurd, but I became ashamed of Jason because he was such an outward and visible sign of all the troubles in my family. I was already trying to keep my friends away from my mother who would shed so many tears and talk about her problems, and I couldn't let them hear my father coming home in the evening, his clock-chiming cough ringing out a warning as he approached. Now I didn't even want them to meet my dog, who rolled his red eyes and ran away if you called him and might bite if you reached out a hand to stroke him.

When my parents finally decided to get a divorce, my father left the house and Jason stayed on with me and my mother. To my amazement, he calmed down almost immediately and only growled if he happened to be close to a stick or a ball and sensed that you might want to take it from him. Apart from that he seemed quite happy.

My father seemed quite happy as well. Within a couple of months he had found himself a new wife and soon after that he'd got a new dog: a stiff-legged and stiff-haired, black-and-white Parson Jack Russell who bore the name of Henry. Henry was already three years old. He was very used to the ways of the world and he had his own priorities about what mattered and what didn't matter in life.

I admired Henry for his formality and independence. He was not in the least concerned with that nonsense about staying to heel or fetching things or waiting for instruction about what to do next. If no one offered to take him for a walk, then he would wait by the front door

Henry

to be let out and he'd set off on his own, always looking carefully both ways before crossing main roads.

But what impressed me most was his relationship with my father. There was no fear and no rage between them. Man and dog were courteous and friendly and treated each other like equals. And if my father started to drink too much, which he still did from time to time, then Henry would watch as the bottles were opened and the glasses were filled, with a look of severe disapproval on his black-and-white face.

At a certain point, when the limit had been passed, the dog would withdraw under a table and stay there, feigning sleep, with his head resting on his paws, and nothing, not even breast of chicken, would persuade him to come out.

But most important as far as I was concerned, Henry bore no grudge. On the mornings after the nights before, when my father was filled with remorse and a headache and plans to stop drinking for ever, Henry would be there to welcome him with his lopsided smile and a little dance of delight.

and treated each other like equals

My father and stepmother rented a cottage in Wales. It was one in a row of dark slate and granite houses, which stood shoulder to shoulder and looked as if they were part of the complex jigsaw of a city slum, except that on all sides they were surrounded by the swelling waves of hills and mountains, the silence broken only by the bleating of sheep, the cries of rooks.

Henry liked it there. He even had a couple of holidays in Wales, all on his own. He stayed in the cottage and let himself out through a large cat flap and he was fed once a day by a neighbour. He was seen every morning setting out on little excursions into the rolling hills. His only problem was the ewes, which often ran towards him bleating enthusiastically, having caught sight of him, lamb-sized and woolly white, and mistaken him for one of their own straying children.

In the last years of his life, my father became so heavy and uncertain on his feet that he couldn't find anyone to go rock climbing with him in the mountains, simply because no one in their right mind wanted to be attached by a long rope to such a dangerous liability. And so Henry became my father's mountaineering companion. They'd set off together, both grinning the same sort of grin.

When they got to the start of a climb, Henry would have one end of the rope tied to a little harness around his shoulders. He would wait patiently while my father struggled heavily up the first stage of the rock face, until he was ready to call to the dog to follow him. If the going became too difficult, then Henry would be untied and put into a rucksack, so he could complete the climb riding on my father's back. I can remember the jubilation in both their faces when they returned from one of these expeditions.

Henry reached some venerable dog age and then one night he died in his sleep, quietly and without fuss. I had a dream about him. In my dream I threw a stick for him and he sat down very solemnly and looked up at

me and said, 'Too far,' in a gruff doggish voice. I thought
it was exactly the sort of thing he might have said, had
speaking been a possibility.

and so Henry
became my father's
mountaineering companion

Talking with Pigs

There are a lot of pigs near where I live. Not pigs jumbled together in the squealing darkness of long metal sheds, but pigs in fields, taking mud baths, chewing at pebbles and sitting together in convivial groups. You see them staring vaguely at the landscape and gossiping, so it would seem, or perhaps they are only discussing the weather.

It must be the nakedness of pigs that makes them appear so human. In the fields they are like a gathering of fat aunts and uncles having a jolly holiday at a nudist camp. And their eyes could be ours as well, the same shape, the same curled lashes and nothing of the blank devil-stare of goats, or the deep dark pools from out of which horses and cows gaze at the world.

I kept pigs for a while, when I lived on a farm with my long-ago husband and our two young children. We had an acre of garden surrounded by hedges and the monotony of wheat fields beyond the boundary. We had two ponds and a crack willow tree which blew down in a storm. We had an sonion bed and a potato patch and rows of French beans and broad beans and runner beans that grew so tall they demolished their own climbing frames. We had free-ranging chickens carefully pecking the heads off the flowers in the herbaceous border and free-ranging guinea pigs whistling to each other through the long grass; and a dog which never growled and a marmalade cat which never scratched and a Muscovy duck which ate dead mice if it found them and followed the cat everywhere, paddling behind it like an incongruous but enthusiastic shadow. We had two white doves that flew in diminishing spirals out of the sky to settle on your hand like a magician's trick when you called for them. And we had pigs.

The pigsty was already there, a solid red-brick dwelling, with its own outside yard. It had been abandoned long ago, but was still in good order. The farmer, who had lived on this same farm when he was a child, was keen that I should try pigs. He said they were easy to look after and good company. 'They're just like family, if you know what I mean,' he said.

I nodded my head as if I understood what he meant, although I hadn't a clue. For me the idea of ease and good company didn't in any way combine with my childhood recollections of family life. But, for the sake of nostalgia for something I had never known, I agreed to try pigs.

A few weeks later the farmer arrived with two piglets in a hessian sack in the back of his truck. I had prepared their beds of straw and the heavy, round cast-iron troughs that can't be knocked over were ready with food and water. Our pigs were decanted into their new home. They were timid and yet already curious. They sat in the sunlight and blinked through pale eyelashes. They suddenly both of them reminded me of my Great-Uncle Guy.

I hadn't been very close to Great-Uncle Guy, but I had been very fond of him. He was the only person genetically related to me who had seemed like Family in the traditional sense of the word and it was from him that I had learnt to

Our pigs were decanted into their new home

enjoy the pleasure of talking about nothing in particular at great length. I now welcomed the piglets and looked forward to getting to know them better.

After my parents separated, I moved upstairs, into my father's old study. I felt it was essential to grow up as quickly as possible and, as a first step on this ladder, I gave away my tropical fish along with the tank and I ceased to be interested in the lives of guinea pigs or the moods of cats and dogs.

Now that there was a spare room in the house, my mother took in a succession of male lodgers. I watched as a procession of total strangers arrived with their belongings, ate at our table, washed in our bathroom and then disappeared without trace.

I felt very uneasy in the company of these random bachelors and did my best to avoid talking to them. Bob the architect who went to Africa and died in a plane crash, was followed by Richard the American painter who walked with a limp and never paid the rent. There

I felt it was essential
to grow up as quickly as possible

was a man who wore sandals all through the winter and then there was Paul from Switzerland who was suffering from a broken heart, which was why he collected naughty magazines and stayed in bed for much of the day and sat up all night in the kitchen, smoking and drinking brandy. He was there every morning when I went down to get my breakfast before going to school. He'd be wearing a white towelling dressing gown, his elbows resting on the round mahogany table, a glass of Courvoisier in his hand and the air thick with the blue haze of French cigarette smoke.

But everything changed on the day when Great-Uncle Guy became our new lodger. Great-Uncle Guy was a relative, a member of our family, the brother of my mother's mother. He was in London to have treatment for throat cancer, but he lived in Malta and had been something in the Navy, although he was now retired. 'He lives with his gardener,' my mother said, and showed me a photograph to prove it. I thought Great-Uncle Guy and the gardener looked very happy in the photograph and the garden looked lovely.

Great Uncle Guy and the gardener looked very happy

Great-Uncle Guy had soft pink skin, pale wispy hair and watery blue eyes. He dressed colonial-style in white flannels, a little straw hat set at a jaunty angle and a red silk scarf tied around his neck, to hide the effects of radiotherapy. He kept to his room, except for meals, when he would come and sip at a glass of sherry and make conversation. He'd mostly talk about the weather and the latest news he'd heard on the radio, although sometimes he talked about his childhood and how boring it had been.

I loved to listen to him and I found that I could talk to him as well. It didn't have to be about anything in particular, and there was no need to steer away from difficult subjects or sudden quarrels or misunderstandings. Conversation with Great-Uncle Guy was about friendliness and a sense of sharing the fact of being alive. 'How was school? Lovely day. Raining this morning. Bought the paper. Egypt's in trouble. I fed the cat.' On and on in a wonderful stream of ease and simplicity.

Great Uncle Guy's hospital treatment lasted for about six months and then he returned to Malta. After a while we received a very formal letter from the gardener, saying that his much-respected employer had died. He enclosed another photograph of the two of them together. Great-Uncle Guy was still looking happy even though his clothes had become far too big for him. It was only years later, when I was living on the farm and keeping pigs, that I was reminded of him and the talks we had had together. It was then I realised how much I had missed him when he was gone.

That farm in the middle of the wheat fields was the first place in my life where I really felt at home. It was partly to do with the house and the garden, the way the morning light came in through the windows, the wild daffodils, the sound of owls hooting in the darkness. It was also to do with having two young children growing up in the company of chickens and guinea pigs, ducks and dogs and cats and doves. But most especially it was because of the pigs.

At first I kept them in their house, but then I began

experimenting with pig freedom. I remember opening the gate and how the two of them gave me a questioning stare, before carefully tiptoeing out into the wider world, uttering little muted shouts of excitement. They were by nature obedient. They would follow at my heels through the fields, running if I ran, and coming to a stuttering halt when I stopped. And if I sat down, they would settle on their fat backsides and look at the landscape with an expression of genial perplexity. I remember planting some willow saplings to thicken up a hedge, with two pigs watching my every move, their mouths slightly open, as if in amazement.

On one occasion I forgot to close the gate to the sty in the evening and early the next morning I looked out of the window to see two fat naked bodies zigzagging joyfully and shamelessly across the lawn, which they had been trampling with their sharp feet and digging into with their strong noses. And then there was the time when I mixed their evening meal with a bit too much of the lees from some beer we were making. They ate with even

I began experimenting with pig freedom

more enthusiasm than usual, and did a wild dance when it was finished. In the morning they didn't come to greet me, but lay on their beds of straw, eyes closed, snoring heavily. For a moment I thought they must be ill, but then I realised they had been drunk and now they simply had bad hangovers and needed time to recover.

Keeping pigs brought its own social life. It was as if I had become a member of an elite club. Local people who had also kept pigs in the days when everyone worked on the land and grew vegetables and had a pig or two, started to drop by. These visitors wouldn't come knocking at the door, but I'd see them standing by the pigsty and I'd go to join them there. There is a way of talking around pigs that is different to other talking. You stand beside the sty and you look at the pigs and the conversation drifts. The pigs take part. Their eyes move to the one who is speaking and with such concentration that they seem to be listening. If someone laughs suddenly, they snort with surprise. The talk is so easy and quiet, drifting without complexity.

gossiping...

or reading the Sunday papers

The farmer who had lived here when he was a child told me about the old way of life and how poor everyone had been. His family used to borrow farm tools from their neighbours and work with them all through the night, so as to return them first thing in the morning. The old bicycle repair man, who had bought his house with the money he made selling mole-skins, talked about the last war and how he hardly ever went to school because his parents needed him for crow scaring; either that or collecting flints from the fields.

The double-jointed man who used to make coffins, but now mended shoes instead, was the only one who wasn't interested in the past. He wanted to tell me about a Certain Lady Recently Widowed, who he thought might agree to marry him. Then there was the very, very old couple who had lived in the farm next to ours years ago and they talked about their pigs. They hadn't kept the more usual Gloucester Old Spots or Large Whites, but those sharp-nosed, red-bodied pigs called Tamworth Reds, and they had walked with them through the fields just as I did. The

The farmer told me about the old way of life

memory made the old lady cry. She said she once had an orphaned Tamworth Red who was so weak everyone said he couldn't last. Night after night she'd put him in the warm bread oven, and that did the trick, that pulled him through.

Even when my mother came to see me, much fatter and quieter by now, we could talk more easily in the company of the pigs. We'd talk about the weather, about things we'd heard on the radio; she'd even remember snatches of her childhood which she had never mentioned before. We never spoke of the lodgers, but we did speak of Great-Uncle Guy and we both said how fond of him we had been and how nice it was, when he came to stay. And all the time the two pigs listened to everything and nodded their heads in easy agreement.

*Night after night she'd put him in
the warm bread oven*